A special gift for

_____

with love,

_____

date

_____

God, God, what do You see?

I see a mother looking at Me.

nspirational Stories to Encourage a Mother's Heart

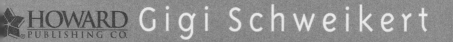

HOWARD PUBLISHING CO. Gigi Schweikert

Our purpose at Howard Publishing is to:
•Increase faith in the hearts of growing Christians
•Inspire holiness in the lives of believers
•Instill hope in the hearts of struggling people everywhere
Because He's coming again!

Published by Howard Publishing Co., Inc.
3117 North Seventh Street, West Monroe, LA 71291-2227
www.howardpublishing.com

05   06   07   08   09   10   11   12   13   14   10 9 8 7 6 5 4 3 2 1

Edited by Between the Lines
Interior design by Stephanie D. Walker and Tennille Paden
Photography by Chrys Howard

Library of Congress Cataloging-in-Publication Data
Schweikert, Gigi, 1962–
    God, God, what do you see? : I see a mother looking at Me / Gigi Schweikert.
        p. cm.
    "The Motherhood Club, making a difference one kiss at a time (MC)".
    ISBN: 1-58229-471-2
        1. Motherhood—Religious aspects—Christianity—Meditations. I. Title.

BV4529.S38 2005
242'.6431—dc22

                                                                        2005046116

To God,
who sees love and strength
in every mother

Contents

Acknowledgments

There are people in our lives who help to shape the mothers we are and the ones we want to be. I have been blessed with so many of those positive influences:

Thanks to my wonderful husband, Al, who gladly carts around our four young children with only a few wipes and an extra diaper.

My eternal love and appreciation to my children, Ashley, Genevieve, Marielle, and William, who are made of love and forgiveness. I'm certainly not the perfect parent, yet they let me off the hook all the time.

Thanks to my parents, Ray and Jean Taylor, for their love, and especially my father, who proved that you're never too old for a miracle.

My grandmother, Mary Abernathy, writes everyday, without a computer. What an inspiration.

Acknowledgments

To my mother-in-law, Theresa Schweikert, who raised eleven children and found the treasure in every one.

To all those who inspired these stories—my husband; Jill and her special Molly; Renee and Sienna; Susan Brenner; and my brother, David.

A special note of appreciation to Dawn and Tammy, my virtual moms at Between the Lines, who are full of love, patience, and great knowledge. They edited every word and made each story real.

Thanks also to Philis and Denny Boultinghouse, from Howard Publishing, who saw and valued the treasure God placed in me.

Thank you as well to all the working moms, at home and in the office. Most of all, thank You, God, for the gift of motherhood and the strength to do more than I could ever imagine.

Love never gives up, never loses faith, is always hopeful,
and endures through every circumstance.

1 Corinthians 13:7 NLT

Introduction

God, God, what do You see? Ever wonder what God sees when He looks down on our homes? He probably doesn't see the piles of laundry or the dishes in the sink, the paperwork that needs sorting or our To Do lists with so many things left undone. No, God sees the love in our hearts. He sees the desire of every mother to comfort and care for her children.

As we gaze into the faces of our lovely children, we realize that every child is a miracle from God. Yet it takes a mother's love to set into motion the miracle God has begun. At times we may feel unworthy of this precious role of motherhood. But God places the perfect child in the arms of the perfect mother. We are those mothers.

With the love we have for our children and the love God has for us, anything is possible.

A Mother's Encouragement

Where your treasure is, there your heart will be also.

Matthew 6:21

God, God, what do You see?

I see a mother
trusting in Me.

A mother's love perceives
no impossibilities.
Cornelia Paddock

The Key

It was the first day of eighth grade, and already Buddy had gotten off to a bad start with yet another teacher.

"I've read your record, Buddy Schroeder." Miss Epple, the stern-faced science teacher, singled Buddy out for no discernible reason. "I'll put up with none of your nonsense this year," she warned him in front of the whole class. "I'll make a respectable young man out of you before this year's through."

Buddy tried not to upset Miss Epple, but eventually he fell into his old patterns: doodling on his papers, looking out the window, and turning in assignments for which he hadn't followed directions. "I'm losing my patience with you, young man," Miss Epple would say to Buddy almost every day.

The tense teacher-student relationship between Miss Epple and Buddy finally exploded when he turned in his paper on amoebas, the single-cell organism of basic biology. Unlike most school assignments, this particular subject actually inspired Buddy. Miss Epple instructed the students: "View an amoeba under the microscope at school, study the labeled illustration of the amoeba in your textbook, and for homework draw a larger-than-life, labeled replica on the white paper I'm giving you."

Then she turned to Buddy. "Do you understand the assignment, Mr. Schroeder?"

Buddy nodded.

"Remember to follow my directions."

Buddy spent hours with his own microscope at home, watching the silent movement of the amoebas and contemplating: *Does this single cell survive independently? Is it possible for a single cell to bond with other like cells to produce greater activity?* The constant movement of the amoebas reminded him of his seven brothers and sisters.

Buddy was enthralled. He bought special markers and poster board at the drug store with money he had earned mowing the neighbor's lawn. Instead of one giant organism, Buddy's poster showed a whole colony of labeled amoebas, with lines charting their traffic patterns. He was sure that this project would redeem him in Miss Epple's eyes. When she saw his masterpiece, she would surely appreciate his passion for science and his creativity.

Buddy waited expectantly the morning Miss Epple returned the graded science papers. He anticipated her holding up his poster for all to see, marveling at his hypothesis of amoeba movement and using his work as an example for the rest of the class. And that is exactly what Miss Epple did. She saved his paper for last. "Mr. Schroeder, would you please come to the front of the class?" The moment he had awaited was here. Now everyone would know he was smart and that he was important, not a weirdo. He would be Buddy Schroeder, Honor Roll Student.

But the rest of the morning was a disappointing blur that would inflict lasting damage to Buddy's self-worth and confidence and scar him for years to come. Miss Epple held up Buddy's amoeba-dotted project. Buddy could see the surprise of his classmates as Miss Epple angrily ripped up his poster and let some of the pieces fall to the floor. It felt as if she had chopped off one of his hands. Buddy stood there, eyes downcast. The classroom was silent. Then

Miss Epple turned to Buddy with an anger that made him flinch. "Mr. Schroeder, you'll never amount to anything. You can't even follow directions. Don't set your sights on college, young man. You'll be lucky if you even graduate from high school."

Buddy could see the disgust on her face. She tossed the remaining pieces of his destroyed assignment toward the trash can. The whole class burst into laughter when his rejected ideas knocked over a beaker of water. Miss Epple fished the wet poster board from the puddle of water and dumped the pieces in the garbage as though she were wiping her hands of the entire mess . . . but mostly of him.

The school bell rang, and Buddy ran. He ran through the hall of shuffling teenagers, down the steps to the school's courtyard, and away from the school. *How could a dumb teacher like Miss Epple and a stupid paper make me feel so bad?* Buddy longed to run into the arms of his mother, who had always appreciated his ideas. Once she had let him place a slice of bread between the wall and the radiator for an entire month to watch the progress of mold—despite the awful odor and even when his sister made a fuss. When teachers or other adults had sympathized that it was too bad Buddy wasn't more like his well-behaved brothers and sisters, Buddy's mother always staunchly defended him: "God gave me seven beautiful children, each a unique individual. There is a treasure in each of them, including Buddy. It's my job to find the key that opens that treasure."

Is there really a treasure in me? Buddy wondered. He sure didn't feel like it, but he decided that his mother and God must know more than Miss Epple, and he was determined to find his key.

"What's wrong with me?" Buddy asked his mother after telling her what had happened. "I'm always getting in trouble. Why can't I be more like everybody else?"

She was silent for a moment, but Buddy could tell by the look on her face that she was searching for just the right answer.

"Buddy, remember a few years ago when you switched the sugar and the salt?"

He remembered the experiment, but the memory of his father

spitting coffee across the table and his baby brother spewing oatmeal on his mother only made him more miserable, given the circumstances.

"As you discovered, sugar and salt look alike, but they serve very different purposes. Both are good. What would we do without either? The problem comes when someone wants sugar and finds salt instead. Just because the Miss Epples of the world can't see the value of salt, doesn't mean you should stop being salt, Buddy," she said earnestly. "God made you the way you are for a purpose—and I love you exactly as you are. You see things in exciting new ways. That's a gift. I have great faith that someday that gift will lead you to do wonderful things—formulate a life-changing scientific theory, discover a new planet, or cure cancer or the common cold. Don't let a teacher who can't recognize the value of salt steal that treasure from you."

It wasn't easy being salt in Miss Epple's sugar bowl. Buddy did his best to stay out of her way, and the year finally passed. So did the next year and the next. Although Miss Epple's destructive words often cast shadows of pain and self-doubt that occasionally threatened to derail him, his mother's words and steady confidence in him proved a strong foundation that even Miss Epple couldn't destroy.

Buddy did graduate from high school and then from college—with honors—and finally from medical school. It was his mother, not Miss Epple, who ultimately proved to be right.

As a young doctor, Buddy used his unique way of looking at the world to develop a revolutionary new treatment for stage-three Parkinson's patients. The ravages of the disease were so terrible that many patients contemplated suicide as they neared the point of requiring constant nursing assistance.

Buddy's clinical trials were going well. In this type of experimental procedure, the patient was anesthetized to pain but fully awake so the surgeon could continually assess any neurological complications as the healthy cells were inserted into the brain. The surgeries were highly successful, and even two years out, the Parkinson's patients were experiencing 60 percent less shaking—and a completely functional quality of life.

It was a blessing for Buddy that his mother had helped him

find the key to unlock the treasure within him when few others saw his potential.

Turns out it was lucky for Miss Epple as well.

One day Buddy's mother sent him a clipping from his hometown newspaper. The familiar feelings of resentment, embarrassment, and anger rose within him when he read his old science teacher's name. "After thirty years of teaching, Miss Epple retires," the article announced. His mother had written in the margin of the article that the woman had unmanageable Parkinson's disease, and the shaking prevented her from teaching. She couldn't even hold the chalk to make a simple mark on the chalkboard. "I've heard that she's given up all hope and wants to die," his mother added. "Perhaps you can help her."

Something inside him rebelled against the idea. Miss Epple didn't deserve any help from him. But the seeds of mercy his mother planted in his mind took root over time. Buddy contacted Miss Epple's primary physician and learned that Miss Epple was a good candidate for surgery. Together they made the necessary arrangements for Dr. Schroeder to operate on his former teacher.

Of course the name Dr. George William Schroeder III wouldn't mean anything to Katherine Epple when she heard it. She'd never known him by his given name, only by his nickname, Buddy realized. It was better that way, he decided.

He entered the operating room gowned, masked, and determined to help his patient. She couldn't see him, but he could see her. She still had a strong effect on Buddy. Old feelings of insecurity and helplessness surged through him. But then he realized that things had changed. She was small, frail, and desperately needed his help. He was successful, confident, and accomplished—everything she had said he'd never be. Suddenly he felt at ease.

Throughout the procedure Dr. Schroeder asked Miss Epple questions to alleviate her anxiety and to be sure other areas of her brain were not being adversely affected. The surgery went well.

He smiled as he imagined Miss Epple's reaction when she'd find out that the doctor who had saved her life was the same young man she'd once written off. But it didn't seem that important anymore. Buddy was no longer the little boy who didn't fit in or measure up. He was Dr. Schroeder: a visionary, a scientist, and a healer. With the encouragement and guidance of his mother, he had long since found the key that opened the treasure God held for him.

A Mother's Encouragement

What do we see when we look at our children? Sometimes it's hard to see past the sticky little hands and toy-strewn rooms, the tantrums during family outings, and the constant testing. Yet God has created each child exactly as He intended. Some are obedient and good tempered; others are challenging and emotional. God wants us as mothers to pour our love into His creations and to find the treasure that exists within each one. A mother's love will set into motion the miracle God has begun.

A Mother's Challenge

My frame was not hidden from you when I was made in the secret place. When I was woven together in the depths of the earth, your eyes saw my unformed body.

Psalm 139:15–16

God, God, what do You see?

I see a mother
hoping in Me.

God's works are perfect
in every stage of their growth.
Hannah Whitall Smith

The Hunt

Joan didn't feel like going to the Easter-egg hunt. She stood in her driveway, the weather cold and dreary, and a light drizzle falling. It didn't feel like spring at all. The ground would be wet and muddy from the previous days of rain. Pushing Martha's wheelchair over the grass at the park was difficult enough, but pushing the wheels through the wet mulch and mud would be almost impossible.

Joan knew how the day would go. Sara and Amy, Martha's younger sisters, would be running off in two different directions before Joan could even get the overpriced metal wheelchair out of the back of the minivan and Martha strapped into the vinyl seat. When the whistle blew for the hunt to begin, Sara and Amy would scramble to the fields and gather candy-filled plastic eggs until their baskets overflowed. Martha would just sit there. That's all she could do.

Although Martha was eight years old now, she weighed only fifty pounds and, on a good day, functioned at the developmental level of a one- or two-year-old. Except for a few barely distinguishable words she grunted to her family, Martha couldn't talk. She still wore diapers, and she had no large motor skills, which meant, in sterile doctor-speak, that Martha couldn't walk or crawl or even sit up. The doctors had given Joan a myriad of medical terms and multisyllabic diagnoses to appease her and Jim's need for answers: severe sensory integration delay, cerebral palsy, and degenerative muscle syndrome.

If anyone asked Joan what was wrong with Martha—and few days went by when she wasn't asked at least once by those who were sincerely concerned, rudely curious, or oddity-seeking voyeurs—Joan simply replied, "A severe case of TMU." That answer satisfied most inquisitive snoopers.

TMU was Joan's own diagnosis: Totally Messed Up. She knew it sounded a bit mean, but humor, even if sarcastic, seemed to help lighten the resentment she harbored about Martha's condition and about her own situation. *Why did God make Martha like she is?* Joan often questioned. *Why did He give her to me? Did I do something wrong? Is this some sort of punishment?*

Totally Messed Up didn't just relate to Martha personally; it described Joan's life in general. With Martha around, life was so much more complicated. Endless doctor and hospital visits also meant enormous medical costs that were approaching the million-dollar lifetime maximum allowed by their insurance. What would they do when there was no more insurance money?

Without a simple, definitive diagnosis for Martha's condition, the quest for a medical solution and some quality of life was a challenge. But despite Joan's feelings of self-pity, she had accepted that challenge long ago. With most kids, being a mother meant potty training and teaching them how to ride a bike, read a book, and whatever skills they would need to function as an adult. Parenting Martha meant helping her find another type of life, another way to live. Yet even Joan wasn't sure what that would be.

Right now she was trying to deal with the everyday, and that's where things got really messed up. Joan and her husband argued a lot, probably in part because they had never really talked about how they felt about Martha's birth and her condition. But mostly because they were just tired. The practical realities of caring for Martha while also raising two other daughters were exhausting.

Despite her exhaustion, Joan had trouble sleeping most nights. *Why?* she thought as she lay staring through the dark at the ceiling. When she got up to check on Martha and as she watched her sleeping, she kept asking the same question. *Why, God? This is not what I imagined being a mother would be like.*

Why would You do this to Martha? she railed at God when children at the playground stared at Martha's contorted arms. Diapering an eight-year-old made Joan demand, *What did I do to deserve this? What did Martha do to deserve this?* She had plenty of questions, but very few answers.

The pregnancy had been fine. Martha's birth was a joyous occasion; she was the first grandchild on both sides of the family. Joan's hospital room was filled with the smiles of family and friends, fresh pink flowers, Mylar balloons announcing "It's a girl," and countless baby gifts. Even though Joan had had little prior experience caring for babies, the first few weeks of motherhood, though largely sleepless, were wonderful. Joan fully embraced being a mother. She counted Martha's ten perfect little fingers and toes. The baby nursed well and was comforted easily. Joan remembered rocking Martha in the freshly wallpapered nursery with matching crib sheets, thinking, *This moment, this time with my baby, is perfect. It's all I've ever dreamed of.*

Only Martha wasn't perfect.

"Mommy, can we go? Can we go now?" four-year-old Amy excitedly tugged at Joan's side, anxious for the family to load into the minivan and head out to the Easter-egg hunt. Joan tried to leave the questions and disappointment behind and focus on her children and the hunt. After folding Martha's wheelchair and placing it in the back of the van, Joan carried Martha from the house and strapped her into her special car seat. Jim gathered the three Easter baskets and put Sara and Amy in their car seats.

When they arrived at the playground, the parking lot was full of minivans. Families were streaming out of their vehicles, and children were running off to join their respective age groups, eager to collect the multitude of plastic eggs that dotted the lawn.

"Mom, if you find a gold or silver egg, you get a special prize," six-year-old Sara announced eagerly. "I'm going to find the gold and silver eggs."

Joan pushed Martha in the wheelchair as Jim herded their family from the parking lot to the safety of the playground. A yellow rope cordoned off the sections of the park designated for the hunt. Children lined up, waiting for the mayor to blow the starting whistle. Jim stood on the sideline near Sara and Amy. The whistle blew, and all the children ran. All but Martha.

Joan thought she seemed content though, watching the flurry of basket-toting kids. She picked up a few brightly colored eggs for Martha and jiggled them in front of her so she could hear the jellybeans rattling inside, then dropped them in Martha's basket with a nice kerplop. Martha turned her head toward Joan. "Do you like the eggs, Martha?" she asked and kissed Martha's head. Joan had never seen Martha smile, but she seemed happy.

Joan turned to watch Sara and Amy clamor for the gold and silver eggs. All the children were running and having so much fun, and she longed for that same kind of fun for Martha—and for herself.

As she turned back to Martha, she saw another child putting eggs into Martha's basket from her own collection. Joan must have looked a bit startled, because the child drew back her egg-filled hands as if worried Joan might think she was doing something wrong.

The little girl quickly explained: "I just thought that since she couldn't bend down and get the eggs herself that I would give her some of mine."

"Oh, thanks, honey," Joan smiled with genuine warmth and appreciation. "I'm sure Martha will like that." The little girl placed another egg in Martha's basket, and Martha seemed to smile. At least it kind of looked like a smile, and that was good enough for Joan. The little girl's mother came over to find her. "Thanks for giving Martha some of your eggs," Joan said to the little girl.

"I want to thank *you*," the girl's mother said, holding out her hand to shake Joan's. "I'm Susan."

Joan gave her a puzzled look, and Susan explained. "I've always admired you. I've seen you at the school and at town events. I'm just so impressed with the way you handle Martha and always take her everywhere you go. You're so loving and patient with her. You inspire me."

Is she kidding? Joan was thinking. *Me, loving and patient? An inspiration?*

Susan kept talking. "You have such a good sense of humor about things. I guess I just wanted to let you know that what you do, the way you act with your daughter, really helps me. I have a child with special needs, too, but I never take him anywhere. I guess I'm a little ashamed, and I can't stand people staring."

Joan knew exactly how Susan felt. For a time she had kept Martha at home too. But she had grown as a mother. Now she felt gratified and grateful to know that the way she was with Martha was helping other mothers.

That night when the jellybeans were gone and the children

were all sleeping, Joan went to each child's bed to give them one more kiss. She lingered over Martha, watching her calm, outstretched limbs. Without her wheelchair she looked perfect. And at that moment, like the time in the nursery when Martha was a newborn, Joan realized that Martha was perfect—different, but perfect. She was just the way God made her. And before Joan could ask the usual, *Why me, God?* she realized a startling truth: God had chosen her to be Martha's mother exactly because she was loving, patient, persistent, and a little wacky. He knew she'd need to be. *He picks the perfect mother for each perfect child,* she at last understood. *And a special child like Martha needs a special mother like me.*

A Mother's Challenge

Not every child is perfect in the world's eyes. As mothers we pray that our children will be healthy and normal, but sometimes they're not. When our children aren't what we expected, we question ourselves and we question God. Being a mother can be difficult. Being a mother of a special child can feel impossible. But we know that God places the perfect child in the arms of the perfect mother. We are those mothers.

A Mother's Time

Childhood and the prime of life are fleeting.
Ecclesiastes 11:10 NASB

God, God, what do You see?

I see a mother
resting in Me.

Children are the anchors
that hold a mother to life.
Sophocles

The Book

Carrie was headed up the basement stairs with a laundry basket full of warm clothes. She always marveled at the worn depressions in each of the fourteen wooden steps leading to the kitchen of her old home. *How many other women have climbed these same stairs over the past century, doing wash or other chores for their families?* she wondered. Enough to wear down the wood. By the time her two-year-old son Jason was grown, Carrie anticipated that the steps would need to be replaced. She once calculated the time she'd spend doing laundry over the next twenty years and had come up with a whopping eight months. Most of her friends told her she had underestimated.

Jason stood at the top of the stairs wearing a bright red, plastic fireman's hat and toting his favorite book, *Silly, Scary Monsters*. "Read, Mommy. Read, Mommy," he pleaded.

Carrie just wanted to get this pile folded and make a few phone calls before she headed to the grocery store. She'd already fluffed this load in the dryer twice. "In a minute, sweetie. Mommy has to take care of these towels." Book in hand, Jason toddled off to the adjoining sunroom.

Holding the telephone between her ear and shoulder, Carrie folded the last towel, pressed it flat with her hands, and glanced over to see Jason pushing a toy fire truck across the carpet, waiting. She saw him look up at her hopefully, grab his *Silly, Scary Monster* book, and head toward her. "Not now, honey," Carrie whispered with her hand over the receiver. "Mommy's on the phone." Jason pushed the book up on the kitchen desk with Carrie's other papers, covering the telephone bill she was discussing with the customer service representative. She gently nudged it aside, ignoring his pleas and his persistent tugging on her sleeve. She softly touched his back trying to redirect him out to the sunroom.

At last, after ten o'clock that night, the house was finally quiet.

Carrie's husband and son were sleeping, and she was going to bed soon. But first she would check on Jason.

His fire hat was on the nightstand by his bed, and his cheeks were pink from the cozy warmth of his bed. When Carrie bent down to kiss him good night once more, she could smell the pleasant scent of his freshly washed hair and hear the calm, slow breaths of his peaceful sleep. She loved this part of her day.

Carrie then headed downstairs to tidy-up the house before turning off the lights. As she rounded the corner to the kitchen, she could see something wedged behind the desk. It was Jason's book, *Silly, Scary Monsters*. She had never read it to him that day, even though he'd asked many times.

Carrie sat down, pulled out the book, and began to read: "Silly, scary monsters running in the sun. Silly, scary monsters having lots of fun. Silly, scary monsters drinking lemonade. Silly, scary monsters walking in parades." It took less than thirty seconds. *How many times did Jason ask me to read this? How many times was I just too busy?* "In a minute, dear." "Not now, honey."

What was so important that she didn't have thirty seconds to pull her little boy onto her lap, read a book to him, and enjoy a precious moment together? Carrie rested her head on her hand and sat in the quiet. *I promised*, she thought bitterly.

Carrie took the book upstairs, pulled a chair over to Jason's bed, and in a low voice, began to read. When she finished, she watched her sleeping son for a long time. Every day would bring another load of dirty clothes to wash and beds to make, but Carrie knew she would never get to relive these moments with Jason. She bowed her head and prayed silently: *God, don't let me get so caught up in the rush of the day that I forget to stop and spend time with my child.*

During the following weeks, Carrie tried hard to spend more time talking and playing with Jason. Whenever she zipped up his coat, she sang, "Zippity-do-da, zippity-ay, I'm zipping up your coat today." And she'd end with a big kiss on his head. *Hey, I've got to put his coat on anyway,* Carrie thought. *I might as well make it fun.*

She even served up Mommy's Extraordinary Eggs for breakfast, even though Jason could only pronounce, "Mommy's Ordinary Eggs"—and that's exactly what they were. But Jason enjoyed all her silly, made-up food names, like Gooey Grilled Cheese and Perfect Peanut Butter and Jelly. When Carrie served him a bowl of plain spaghetti, she picked up one long noodle and held it above his giggling, upturned face, feeding it to him a little at a time. "Here's your bowl of yummy worms, baby bird. I want you to eat them all up." Jason grinned and finished every "worm."

The next time Carrie was hauling the fresh laundry up to the kitchen, she saw Jason at the top of the stairs again. "Read, Mommy. Read the book," he pleaded, *Silly, Scary Monsters* book in hand. Carrie started to skirt around him with the usual, "In a minute, honey," but she caught herself and instead told Jason to follow her into the sunroom. To Jason's surprise and delight, Carrie dumped the whole basket of fresh-smelling clothes on the sunroom carpet. She laid down in the middle of the pile and pulled Jason onto her stomach. With shared glee they rolled around in the assortment of warm clothes.

Then Carrie grabbed the book, helped Jason find a comfortable spot in the pile, and read: "Silly, scary monsters running in the sun. Silly, scary monsters having lots of fun. Silly, scary monsters drinking lemonade. Silly, scary monsters walking in parades."

She read it again and again. "More, more," Jason said after each reading. Then they paraded into the kitchen like silly, scary monsters and drank lemonade.

Days like these passed too quickly. So did the years. "Children grow up so fast," Carrie had heard her mother say repeatedly. "It seems like only yesterday that you were just a little girl yourself." Even Carrie's husband would remind her after trying days, "He won't be little forever." Still she was amazed when she looked back at how quickly the years had flown.

Today, decades later, when Carrie looked back again, she had been gathering up years of memories in boxes before moving. Her husband had recently died, and Carrie wasn't comfortable living in the old house alone. A young couple was moving in tomorrow, and today Jason was coming over to help her pack up the last of her things. It had been an emotionally and physically exhausting week. Yet despite how tired she was each night, Carrie had had difficulty falling asleep. When she finally did, it was a restless sleep at best. This morning she had awakened at sunrise, then drifted back to sleep thinking about the day ahead.

Carrie thought she could hear Jason calling her from the other room. "Read, Mommy, read." She could picture him dressed in his pajamas with the red, plastic fire hat perched on his head, disheveled blond hair peeking out. But she realized she was only dreaming. Jason was thirty years old now and had a son of his own.

She went into Jason's old room and stood thinking about the basket of toys he'd kept by his bed. The basket had been filled with matchbox cars, a collection of stuffed animals, and lost puzzle pieces. Carrie thought about Jason's sports trophies that lined the shelf her husband had built. She could almost smell the fresh sheets she used to put on his bed and feel the way she'd tucked in the corners.

Carrie realized that Jason's childhood had been just a collection of simple moments. "Thank you, God, for helping me to enjoy those times with my son," Carrie said aloud, then sighed wistfully. Time to get dressed and finish her packing.

Carrie was in the basement washing curtains when Jason and his son, Colin, arrived. Carrie's friends were right. She'd definitely spent more than eight months of her life doing laundry—but it was worth every minute, especially when she dumped a fresh load on Jason. Even when he was in high school, Carrie would pour the warm laundry over his head while he watched TV.

Carrie was heading up the steps, taking comfort in the familiar depressions of the worn wood, when she saw her three-year-old grandson at the top of the stairs, holding a book. "Read this, Nana. Read this." The image reminded her of Jason twenty-eight years earlier. She was delighted to recognize the book: *Silly, Scary Monsters*. Colin must have fished it out of one of the boxes.

"Hey, I remember that book from when I was a kid," Jason said as he put down the box he was holding. Carrie watched as Jason told Colin, "Not now, honey. We have to finish helping Nana. We'll read later." Colin held up the book, again pleading, "Read, Nana, read."

"Oh, it'll just take a minute," Carrie said as she sat down on a sturdy box. Jason and Colin sat on the floor in front of her, and Carrie held the book so they could all see the pictures. "Silly, scary monsters running in the sun. Silly, scary monsters having lots of fun. Silly, scary monsters drinking lemonade. Silly, scary monsters walking in parades." Her son and grandson looked up at her with smiles, and Carrie gave silent thanks for yet another precious moment with her child.

A Mother's Time

As mothers we find it difficult to shut out the world or even just slow down the whirling activity in our homes. We focus on the chores of life, often ignoring the women who have made their child's last school lunch and kissed their child's last skinned knee. "They grow up before your eyes," they tell us. Somehow we think it'll be different for us. But the simple moments with our children can be easily lost. Let's not leave God's gifts behind.

A Mother's Loss

*Trust in the LORD with all your heart
and lean not on your own understanding.*

Proverbs 3:5

God, God, what do You see?

I see a mother
leaning on Me.

Ultimately mourning means facing what wounds us
in the presence of One who can heal.

Henri Nouwen

Letting Go

Beth remembered every detail about her son's life.

He was born with white-blond hair, and his smile seemed to say, "I'm going to get into everything." Which he did. Even as a baby, Sam was adventurous. Beth would find him pulling up on the kitchen chairs and then hoisting himself up on the counter for a bird's-eye view of the room—before he could even walk.

Each time she rescued him from his latest climbing conquest, Beth would put him back on the floor and say, "Mommy doesn't want you to fall, honey. Play down here." But Sam never stayed on the floor. Within minutes he would be climbing something else.

Beth tried a playpen with extra-high sides, a crib with a mesh top, and a maze of gates that only served to trip her husband when he tried to clear the hurdles. But nothing worked with Sam. "This kid is like a little Spider-Man," Beth told her husband. "He can climb anything."

When Sam was in elementary school, Beth watched him climb tall maple trees in the backyard. In middle school Sam started rappelling the back ravines of the Appalachian Mountains on weekends with the church youth group. And when Sam jumped out of an airplane as a teenager, Beth waited on the ground with trepidation.

Like any mother, Beth was concerned about her son, but she never discouraged him. On the contrary, despite her fears, she was Sam's greatest cheerleader. She knew the thrill Sam got from the heights, the speed, and the beauty of nature.

Those thrills sometimes had consequences, but Beth was always there when Sam needed her. When Sam was five years old, she had to climb a tree in the park to rescue him. He had climbed almost to the top but was too frightened to come down.

When Sam was ten, he and his friends built a ramp for their bikes. Through the living-room window, Beth watched them barrel down the street, gaining speed, then make a sharp right turn into the driveway and take the plywood ramp as fast as they could peddle. The grass on the other side of the ramp was worn away—and so was the skin on Sam's knee, from the tumble after his bike hit the side of the ramp instead of the end.

But Beth didn't scold him. She just calmly reminded Sam, "Be careful, honey," then brought out plenty of lemonade and freshly baked cookies for all the boys. She overheard one of Sam's friends say, "Your mom's cool," and a smile came to her face when she saw Sam nod in agreement as he shoved another chocolate-chip cookie in his mouth.

Each night Beth would slip into Sam's room for a final check. She'd lean down and kiss his soft cheek, then quietly pray: "Dear God, thank You for the precious gift of my child. Help me to be the best mother I can be. Give me more love, grace, patience, and mercy. Help me be a good mother to Sam."

But I wasn't there when Sam needed me most. The tormenting thought often disrupted her happy memories. *I didn't keep him from dying.*

When Sam got older, Beth wasn't surprised or disappointed

that he selected a college based on its reputation for recreational opportunities rather than its reputation for academic excellence. "This college has everything," he said excitedly. "Great hiking and rock climbing, skiing in the winter, and swimming in the summer."

"Just be sure you study," Beth reminded him. She couldn't believe how quickly he'd grown. His white-blond hair had darkened to ash blond. His once-soft, chubby hands were the rough, strong hands of a man, and his fair skin seemed permanently tanned from being outdoors in all seasons. But he still seemed like her baby. It wasn't easy to let him go, but she did it.

The day before Mother's Day of Sam's freshman year, Beth felt lonely. It would be her first Mother's Day apart from her son. She found herself wishing she could look out the window and see him speeding around the corner again on his bike. But when she looked out the window, she saw only the mailman. She sighed and headed outside to collect the mail. Between the electric bill and an ad for mattresses, Beth spied a letter from

Sam. She eagerly tore it open. Tears welled up as she read Sam's letter, then read it again, and again.

That evening Beth called Sam to thank him for the note. She didn't want to embarrass him, so she simply said, "Sam, I loved your letter."

"Thanks, Mom," Sam said, sounding pleased. "And thanks for not getting gushy," he added.

Less than a month later, Sam was riding his bike to class when he was hit by a car. He was airlifted to one of the best hospitals in the area, but his head injuries were so severe there was nothing the doctors could do. "Of all the crazy things that kid did in his life . . ." Beth marveled sadly to her husband as they made the frantic, agonizing trip to get to Sam. "To be just riding his bike to school and—" She choked back sobs.

When they got to Sam's bedside, the doctors explained the severity of his condition. He had no brain activity. He couldn't breathe or even regulate his body temperature on his own. There was no hope.

Beth shuddered and broke down as she realized she would have to let her little boy go one final time.

She held his hand until the very end. "Still my baby's hand," she said quietly as she stroked his rough, scraped knuckles, willing herself to memorize every line and how it felt to touch them. The room grew silent. She watched as Sam turned blue, then pale, then still.

After several minutes of watching, willing Sam's chest to heave with one more breath, Beth's husband walked away. But not Beth.

"If only I could have saved you," she whispered to Sam. "I should have protected you. I should have loved you more and helped you more."

The nurse put her arm on Beth's shoulder in a gesture of comfort that Beth didn't want to accept. "No," she said firmly, pulling away from the nurse. "How could I let this happen to my son?"

"It's not your fault," the nurse said kindly. "A car hit him. You couldn't have stopped that."

Beth knew the nurse was right, that she was being unreasonable, but she couldn't stop feeling responsible for Sam's death. It must have been something about the way she'd raised him. If only she hadn't allowed him to take so many risks . . . surely then Sam would still be alive.

After Sam's death the feelings of guilt, grief, and regret were never far from Beth. *I should have made him go to school near home,* she told herself. *If he had lived at home, I could have kept him safe. I should have bought him a car. Then he wouldn't have been riding his bike. I shouldn't have pushed him to take summer classes. I should have let him go on vacation—anywhere—where he would have been safe.*

Years passed, but the wound from the loss of her son never seemed to heal. Beth struggled with her memories, her feelings of guilt, and her grief. She missed Sam terribly, and worse than feeling like she was no longer a mother, she felt like she'd been a bad mother. How else could she explain Sam's death?

Mother's Day was always the hardest, and today was Mother's

Day. When Beth awoke, thoughts of Sam replaced dreams of him. She smiled as she recalled the last Mother's Day Sam had been alive and the precious letter he'd sent her. She hadn't read it since his death—it was just too painful. But today she needed to read it again. She pulled the dog-eared piece of notebook paper carefully from under her jewelry box and unfolded it. Seeing her son's familiar handwriting brought both comfort and heartache. She could almost hear his voice as she read:

> *Dear Mom,*
>
> *Sometimes mothers don't know how wonderful they are.*
> *They wonder whether they said the right things, kissed all the hurts, gave enough hugs, taught the important lessons, spent enough time with their children, and had enough patience with dirty boots and messy rooms.*
> *They worry about whether they played in the sand with their kids, made lemonade, put fresh, warm sheets on the bed, and said I love you.*

*And mothers wonder whether they made the right
decisions.*

You did all those things and more.

Happy Mother's Day!

> *Love always,*
>
> *Sam*

By the end of the letter, tears were streaming down Beth's
cheeks. For the first time in all those years, the weight of guilt
lifted from her heart. She felt Sam's love and forgiveness, and at
last she felt that her healing had begun. There was just one more
thing she needed to do.

Beth took out a piece of paper and a pen and wrote:

Dear Sam,

*As mothers we can teach our children to be polite,
hardworking, and loving, but we can't control what
they become or what happens to them. We can love*

them, pray for them, and wish them success—whatever that is.

I used to think your life should have been more and that I could have helped. But now I know that God has a plan for us all, and even moms can't control that plan. You belong to God. I thank Him for letting me hold your hand as long as I did. I'm so grateful I was able to hold you when you were young and comfort you when you were dying. In spite of all the pain of losing you, I'm so glad you gave me the chance—and God helped me to be a good mother.

Love always,
Mom

A Mother's Loss

For those who have lost a child, life is never the same. As mothers, protecting our children is our primary concern, and when we loose a child, we feel as though we've somehow failed. But that's not true. We don't know why God calls children to heaven ahead of their parents, but He knows. Although the hurt of letting go may always be with us, God is always with us too.

A Mother's Worth

To enjoy your work and accept your lot in life—
that is indeed a gift from God.

Ecclesiastes 5:19 NLT

God, God, what do You see?

I see a mother
following Me.

There is a loftier ambition than merely to stand high
in the world. It is to stoop down
and lift those around us a little higher.

Henry van Dyke

The Choice

"What a sight," Elizabeth said to herself as she glanced at her reflection in the kitchen window. It was almost noon, and she was still dressed in her nightgown. Her hair was pulled back in a ponytail, and her face bore not a trace of makeup except the mascara left under her eyes from yesterday. She didn't think she'd even brushed her teeth today. Cheerios covered the kitchen counter, and stacking rings, stuffed animals, and puzzle pieces were scattered on the family-room floor. Elizabeth was home on maternity leave.

Each morning she struggled with feeling she should be doing more than just staying home all day and taking care of her two children, four-year-old Chelsea and newborn Chloe.

"I have so much more to offer the world than changing diapers and cooing," she said aloud, maybe just to hear an adult voice.

"I have tons of education, great job experience, and I make good money."

No one seemed very impressed when she said she was a mother, but when she said, "I'm an investment banker," heads always turned. She was good at her job. But at home with the kids, she often felt inadequate and overwhelmed. She missed the sense of progress and accomplishment she got from her career. Here it was one step forward, two steps back. Nothing ever stayed clean, no task was ever really finished.

A cassette of Chelsea's kiddie music was playing in the background, and the words of the song struck Elizabeth as appropriate for her own life: "The wheels on the bus go round and round, round and round, round and round." She stood at the refrigerator door, forgetting why she was there, and thinking, *That's what being a mother is like. Just going round and round— only I seem to be getting nowhere.*

Just then the phone rang. Her heart fluttered as she saw on the caller ID that it was her office. She cleared her throat.

"Hello . . . hello," she practiced to make sure she hadn't lost her voice or forgotten how to sound like a professional.

"Hello?"

"Hey, Elizabeth, it's Dawn. How's it going?"

"Oh, Dawn, it's so good to be able to talk to an adult. I hope you've called to get my advice about a situation there at work."

Dawn chuckled. "Not really. But we do miss you. Weren't you the one who thought you'd go straight from the delivery room to the office after this baby? Have you changed your mind and decided to stay home?"

"Are you kidding me? Of course I'm coming back to work. Can you see me home full time with two kids? I'd go nuts. I'm not the stay-at-home type."

"I don't know," Dawn mused. "Now that my kids are grown, I wish I'd been with them more when they were little."

"You'd never have made it as far as executive vice president by putting your career on hold for mothering."

"I suppose you're right, Elizabeth, but somehow I still feel like I missed something more important. I wish I'd traded in the briefcase for the diaper bag when I had the chance."

"Not me!" Elizabeth said emphatically. "I can't wait to get back to the office. I'll be there before you know it."

After an all-too-brief conversation, Elizabeth leaned against the refrigerator and thought back to her first pregnancy. It had been great, just as she'd planned. Elizabeth liked everything planned and in order. That's probably why she was so good with numbers. She'd jotted her due date in her Franklin Planner the same as any meeting or obligation. Elizabeth had assumed that if the doctor told her that was when the baby was due, then that was when the baby would arrive. She'd even cleared the whole day before delivery and the day after. "Three days, and I'll be back at work," Elizabeth had told her co-workers. And technically she was. Elizabeth was checking her voice mail and advising clients from the hospital.

Before the birth Elizabeth and her husband had decorated the nursery with specially ordered crib linens and had even hired an artist to paint a mural depicting the classic children's story *Guess*

How Much I Love You. Elizabeth's friends and family threw her a tremendous baby shower with little pink-and-blue party favors wrapped in toile, and gifts galore: an electronic bouncy seat, remote-controlled baby swing, state-of-the-art ear thermometer, dirty-diaper disposal pail, and clothes—mountains of tiny little clothes, so many that Elizabeth didn't think her baby would be able to wear them all.

Elizabeth had imagined what the birth would be like. Her husband would be at her side holding her hand. The nurses would hand her an angelic, pink-faced baby, and she would immediately fall in love with a little bundle of joy.

But when Chelsea was born, it wasn't at all what Elizabeth had expected. As much as she craved the elation she imagined other new mothers felt, after hours of labor and pushing, all she really wanted was sleep. And when the nurse handed Elizabeth her baby, the infant was wrinkly and bruised from birth. Most alarming and dismaying to Elizabeth was her first reaction to her baby: *She's not really very cute. She's kind of weird looking, not at all like the cherubic faces on the covers of parenting magazines.*

Then came breast-feeding, another of the misrepresented "women have been doing this since before time" mommy skills. Elizabeth had read the books, taken the classes, talked with a lactation consultant, and polled every colleague, friend, and even some strangers about the benefits of bottle versus breast. She'd imagined wearing the beautifully embroidered nursing gown her mother had given her, snuggling her newborn close to her body, and *voila!*

Well, *voila!* didn't happen. When she finally managed to get Chelsea to eat, Elizabeth was usually in some uncomfortable, contorted position, with backaches and shoulder pain, afraid to move a muscle or the baby might stop.

The "love at first sight," "mothering is instinctive" stuff people spouted was a farce as far as Elizabeth could see. She would rather have been in a business meeting with a fresh cup of coffee discussing third-quarter earnings. At least then she'd know what she was doing.

But Elizabeth wasn't at work, she was at home. Her cup of coffee was cold. She'd taken just two sips in two hours, but now at least she remembered why she'd gone to the refrigerator. She opened the freezer, scooped up some ice cubes, and plopped them into her mug. "Now I have iced coffee," she said in a defiant attempt to snatch victory from defeat. Then she shook her head. "And now I talk to myself." Elizabeth raised the cup to take a sip, but just as the coffee was about to reach her lips, Chloe started crying.

Elizabeth closed her eyes and stood still for a minute. Every time she tried to enjoy one simple pleasure—like, say, brushing her teeth—the baby would cry. *I'm convinced babies can hear when their moms start to eat or drink or sleep or even go to the bathroom. It must be some sort of innate, drive-your-mother-crazy, infant survival skill.* She let out a weary half-chuckle. At least she'd get a break when she went back to work in six more weeks. She wouldn't hear the constant "Mommy," she'd get to sit down with other adults and eat lunch—she'd even get to go to the bathroom alone. *Now that's the life*, she thought.

Chloe's newborn cry brought Elizabeth's mind back from the boardroom to the family room. *Another baby*, she thought, shaking her head as she picked up Chloe from the cradle. *What was I thinking? I couldn't get the hang of it with the first one.* She pushed books and toys from the sofa to the floor so she could sit down and feed the baby. "At least I finally figured out how to do this," Elizabeth cooed to the newborn as she snuggled her to her chest. "You won't starve." She looked around at the messy house. *I've gotten absolutely nothing accomplished today—again.*

Soon Chelsea climbed onto the couch and rested her head contentedly on Elizabeth's free arm, studying the new baby. She placed her little hand on the infant's fuzzy head and rubbed it slowly, then touched the baby's toes on each foot.

"Mommy," Chelsea said. "I bet this baby never had such a special family like ours." She snuggled closer, under Elizabeth's arm, and rested her hand lovingly on Chloe's leg. "I'm glad you're home with me, Mommy."

Elizabeth's heart melted with love for her two little girls. *Maybe I'm accomplishing more at home than I realized,* she thought. *But how could I leave all the things I've worked so hard for at the office? I'm the next in line for vice president.*

When Chloe finally went to sleep and Chelsea was engrossed in a video, Elizabeth decided it was time to get dressed. She'd just pulled on a pair of sweatpants, the official uniform of just-given-birth mothers, when the doorbell rang. Elizabeth went to the front door and opened it to find a large box on the small porch. She carried it to the kitchen table, cut through the packing tape to open it, and dug through the foam pieces to find a black leather bag. At first glance she thought it was a briefcase, but upon further inspection, she realized it was a beautiful diaper bag. Inside was a card:

> *In case you're thinking about a trade-in. There really is no job more important than being a mom, not even executive vice president.*
>
> *Love,*
> *Dawn*

Elizabeth ran her fingers over the soft leather and knew her friend was right. She wasn't going round and round like the wheels on the bus. She was raising two children. Her work in the family room was much more important—and at times much more difficult—than her work in the office. Her daily accomplishments were less obvious than third-quarter earnings, but her seemingly simple duties of caring for her children were exactly what she was supposed to be doing. It took her friend and even her four-year-old daughter to help her see that. But God had entrusted Chloe and Chelsea to her care. *Being a mother is, in a way, just like any other job,* she thought. *It's hard work, and it requires learning new skills.* But Elizabeth was starting to realize it was the most wonderful job of all.

A Mother's Worth

As little girls many of us dreamed about having children. But most of us never thought about what it really means to be a mother—sleepless nights, making meals, and endless loads of laundry. There's no course for motherhood in school, which makes sense, because being a mother doesn't seem to mean much in today's world. Yet it means everything to our children. Even if the job doesn't come naturally, we can take God's hand. It was He who chose us to be mothers.

A Mother's Love

*Faith is being sure of what we hope for
and certain of what we do not see.*

Hebrews 11:1

God, God, what do You see?

I see a mother
depending on Me.

There are only two lasting bequests
we can hope to give our children.
One of these is roots; the other, wings.
Hodding Carter III

The Good-Bye

"Can you believe our daughter is graduating from law school today?" Richard whispered to his wife, squeezing her hand in a way that communicated his pride for his daughter and affection for his wife.

"Of course I can. It's what I've always wanted."

"For Rachel," Emma added quickly when she saw the hint of a frown her comment brought to Richard's face.

Her mind was quickly drawn to other things as she strained to pick out which cap and gown belonged to Rachel among the dozens of graduates seated in the auditorium's front rows. Precious moments from Rachel's childhood flashed through her mind—preschool artwork of small handprints, angelic smiles with missing teeth, middle-school squabbles over teenage outfits, and high-school track meets. Every moment had been wonderful, and they had all led to this moment, the culmination of a life of dreams and sacrifice.

"I think you're more excited than Rachel," Richard remarked, bemused. "You'd almost think you were the one graduating today."

"I'm so happy, it feels as if I were!" Emma was so proud of Rachel. She was intelligent, beautiful, kind, and always a great kid. Rachel had gone to law school right after college, something Emma had always wanted to do.

As Rachel's name was called and she started her walk across the platform, Emma jumped to her feet clapping and cheering. Richard took advantage of his height to try to get a clear shot with the video camera. Emma beamed as Rachel confidently shook the hand of the robed dignitaries and accepted her hard-won diploma. Emma couldn't help but dream of her daughter's wonderful future, now so close at hand. Undoubtedly Rachel would move closer to downtown Atlanta, take a position with a prestigious law firm, and start pushing her way toward partner.

When Emma found Rachel in the crush of the crowd after

the ceremony, she hugged her daughter tightly. "I'm so proud of you," she whispered, tears spilling into Rachel's hair. "You'll be a wonderful lawyer. You'll have more job offers than you know what to do with," she predicted.

"I hope not." Rachel's voice suddenly seemed strained. "I've already accepted a job offer."

"What?" Emma drew back with a gasp. "Why didn't you tell us? Which firm?"

"We'll talk about it later," Rachel said evasively. "When we get home."

For some reason Emma didn't like the sound of that.

"Are you crazy?" Emma responded that night when Rachel told her and Richard about her new job in the Colorado Rockies. "What about your education? What are you going to do in Colorado?" Emma demanded, her voice rising.

Rachel answered simply, "I'm going to take a break from studying, work the front desk at a ski lodge, learn to ski better, and enjoy the beauty of nature."

Emma was furious. "Now, that's worth $100,000," she said

sarcastically. "You're just going to throw it all away to work at a ski lodge?"

"You've always wanted me to do what *you* want," Rachel shouted back defiantly. "For once I'm doing what I want. Maybe it's the right decision—maybe it's not. But it's *my* decision." She stormed up the stairs to her bedroom. "I'm leaving next week," she yelled down the stairs before shutting the door—loudly.

Distraught, Emma collapsed into the wing chair and turned to her husband. "Why in the world would she choose the Rocky Mountains?"

Richard shrugged. "We went there on a summer trip when Rachel was a teenager," he suggested.

"We went to Disney World once too," Emma snapped. "I'm surprised she didn't get a job there."

A few minutes of silence passed, and Emma's voice softened. "I always wanted Rachel to follow her heart and make her own decisions. When she was a little girl, I always told her she could do anything she wanted when she grew up." Some of her agitation returned. "I should have told her, 'You can do anything you'd like as long as I approve and you don't move away.'" Richard laughed and put his hand on hers. "And what I don't understand," Emma added with a fair amount of pique, "is that I also used to tell her to pick up her dirty clothes. She never listened to me about that! Why is it she's learned the lesson on independence, but she still can't get a dirty sock in the clothes hamper?" And then, without warning, Emma melted into tears.

Every day she prayed that Rachel would change her mind. *If Rachel moves to Colorado,* she thought, *I'll be too far away to drop in with a home-cooked meal. I won't be able to drive to her apartment when she needs advice, or to hold her when she's discouraged. I won't be able to tidy up the place, fill her refrigerator with food, or leave a twenty-dollar bill on the kitchen table so she'll have a little extra money in her pocket.*

After twenty-four years of seeing Rachel almost daily, her little girl had grown up. Emma had just been too busy being her mother to notice. *Did I think I was going to pack her lunch before she headed to her law office every day?* Emma berated herself. *In court the prosecutor could ask her, "What did your mother put in your lunch today? Any of those chocolate-chip cookies?"* She laughed at the caricature of her overly involved behavior. She knew she had to let Rachel go, but it was still difficult. She just couldn't bear to say good-bye.

Emma tried to make the farewell as peaceful as possible. She washed and folded Rachel's clothes, packed a cooler full of snacks and soft drinks, made her favorite breakfast of blueberry pancakes, and organized a folder of directions and emergency numbers to go along with the new cell phone she'd bought for her daughter.

But despite Emma's good intentions, she and Rachel argued. Emma just couldn't help telling her how she felt. They hadn't fought like that since Rachel was a teenager.

"You just don't understand me." Rachel shook her head, exasperated.

"I understand you perfectly," Emma responded. "I'm your mother. You're smart enough to go to law school, but now you're being irresponsible. Your father and I didn't make all those sacrifices so you could follow some wild dream."

"I thought that's exactly why you made those sacrifices, Mom. You've always told me to do what's in my heart—to follow God's leading. Now you're going back on everything you ever taught me. But you know what, it doesn't matter. I'm an adult, and I can do what I want. That's what really makes you mad, isn't it. I'm not your little girl anymore!" With that Rachel slammed the car door and drove away.

Emma wanted to stop her, to hug her, to say good-bye, but she couldn't. She sat on the front steps for half the morning, hoping to see Rachel's car coming back up the driveway. Rachel would get out, fling her arms around Emma, and say, "You were right, Mom. I'm so sorry. What was I thinking? Help me find a job close by, and I'll meet another lawyer, get married, and have grandchildren for you."

That's my dream, not hers, Emma reminded herself. *Where has my little girl gone?* She remembered the time six-year-old Rachel fell in love with a pair of ladies' sandals—strapless high heels with a silver, glittery band in the front and a clear, plastic heel. To Rachel they looked like Cinderella's glass slippers, and she begged

Emma to buy them. She did, and Rachel clip-clopped around in those princess shoes for weeks. It was the only time Emma wished she didn't have hardwood floors. When she tucked Rachel into bed that first night and asked, "Where are your Cinderella shoes?" Rachel threw back the covers to reveal that she was still wearing the high heels, even in bed. "I'll never take them off," she vowed.

She did, of course, but now Emma giggled thinking of Rachel wearing those princess shoes as she hiked up the side of a mountain in Colorado. She had grown out of that phase. Maybe she'll outgrow this one too.

Emma sighed and stood up stiffly, finally ready to go inside. "No matter what," she said, "she'll always be my little girl."

Rachel didn't come back that day. She sent a brief text message to Richard's cell phone, letting him know she had arrived safely in Arkansas, where she would spend the night with a friend from school.

"She must hate me," Emma said miserably to her husband.

"I've ruined everything, and nothing will ever be the same. No wonder she doesn't want to talk to me."

"She doesn't hate you," Richard consoled. "She just needs a little space."

"I didn't want her to go," Emma said wearily. "I wanted her to get a good job close to home, meet a nice man, get married, and have children. That's what I wanted."

"But is that what Rachel wanted?" Richard gave Emma a loving embrace, then wiped her tears with his thumbs. "You've been a great mother. You'll always be her mother, but now it's time for our little girl to make her own decisions. She's all grown up."

"I suppose you're right," Emma agreed reluctantly. "It's been a long day. I'm going to bed." Emma went upstairs, but she paused at the door to Rachel's bedroom. Suddenly she needed to go inside—to look at the things Rachel had left behind and smell the fragrance of her daughter that lingered on the sheets and in the air.

On the pillow of Rachel's bed was a crisp, pink envelope

addressed simply, "Mom." Emma picked up the note and hurriedly opened it.

> *Dear Mom,*
>
> *I'm not leaving you—I'm going to find me. You'll always be my mom, and I'll always be your little girl. I love you.*
>
> *Rachel*

Emma held the note to her chest as if she were embracing her daughter. When she could finally speak, her voice was soft and choked with emotion. "Good-bye!"

A Mother's Love

As our children grow to be adults, we want them to be happy and successful. Sometimes we long for them to follow in our footsteps, live our unfulfilled dreams, or have what we never did. Although as mothers we'll always have influence, we can't control the actions of our grown children. In spite of our wishes to keep them little, the time comes when they must make their own decisions. We nurture them under our wings, but we must also release them to fly. God wants us to let them soar.

A Mother's Presence

As a mother comforts her child,
so I will comfort you.
Isaiah 66:13

God, God,
what do You see?

I see a mother
believing in Me.

The angels . . . singing unto one another,
can find among their burning terms of love,
none so devotional as that of mother.
Edgar Allen Poe

The Gift

It was her mother's birthday. This would be the first year Susan would spend it alone.

She stepped onto the sidewalk from the shelter of her apartment building and was hit by a strident, wet wind that cut through her thin coat like a knife. The gray, stormy day matched her mood. Her heart didn't feel like dancing, and her determination wavered. Maybe she'd just go back inside, stay in bed all day, pull the covers up over her head, and hide from the world today. But no, Susan's mother had always supported her dream to dance ballet professionally. She would want Susan to go ahead with that dream—to succeed.

Normally she would have walked the twenty blocks to the theater where the audition was being held. She loved taking long strides up Fifth Avenue and cutting over to Central Park. But the threatening weather and the bitterness in her soul made the trek seem daunting. She decided to hail a cab. She stepped off the curb, threw up her arm, and yelled, "Taxi!" A yellow cab turned the corner and pulled up beside her as if on cue. Susan opened the car door, slid across the backseat, and settled in.

What am I doing? She wondered about her uncharacteristic decision to ride. *I probably should have walked—the traffic is heavy. But I guess there's plenty of time before the audition.*

"Where to?" the driver asked.

"Avery Fisher Hall," Susan responded softly.

"Don't seem too excited about going to a show," he remarked. Their eyes met in the rearview mirror. He seemed to be studying her.

"I'm not going to a show," Susan explained. "I'm auditioning to become a member of a ballet company."

"You're a dancer?" He sounded impressed. "Are you famous? You look kind of familiar. My wife always likes to know if I have a celebrity in the car."

The mention of his wife made Susan feel more at ease about

his interest in her, as did the genuine warmth and kindness in his voice.

"Oh no," Susan said self-consciously. "I've never danced professionally before—and I may never if I don't ace this audition."

"You will." The cabbie smiled back at her. "I've got a good feeling for you. Like someone upstairs is looking out for you. Today you're going to charm them."

The man's words brought a jumble of conflicting emotions. He couldn't know her situation or the significance of the words he was saying, but their encounter seemed almost providential—a much-needed reminder that she was not alone. Her mother had always told her that angels were watching over her. And the word *charm* unleashed a flood of memories, especially on this special day, her mother's birthday. She leaned back and closed her eyes to signal the cabbie that she didn't want to talk, and she let the memories sweep her away.

Each year for her mother's birthday, Susan's father had given her mother a charm to add to the bracelet he'd given her when they first came to America from Romania. At first the bracelet held only one charm, a small replica of the Statue of Liberty. A tiny replica gift box was the next trinket added to the bracelet, and a little rattle followed that.

For every charm there was a story. When she was a child, Susan would choose a dangling emblem from the bracelet, and her mother would tell her the tale behind it. Susan would plead excitedly, "Tell me the story about the Statue of Liberty!"

"The Statue of Liberty stands for freedom," her mother would begin, and then she would tell Susan about how she and her father had come to America to have freedom.

When Susan asked to hear the story about the gift charm, she would hear how her mother and father had anxiously waited for God to send their family a very special gift.

"What kind of gift, Mommy?" Susan would question, already knowing the answer.

"Let's unwrap the gift and see," her mother would reply. She'd hold Susan tight, pretending she was a package wrapped in fancy, flowered paper with a fabulous pink bow. "What a beautiful package from God. What could be in this lovely wrapping? Is it the gift I always dreamed of?" Slowly untying the pretend pink ribbon and placing it carefully on the bed, Susan's mother would then start to peel the imaginary wrapping paper from around Susan and exclaim, "My special gift! My baby girl has come." And then she would rip off the remaining pretend paper and tickle Susan until her sides ached from laughter.

There was a tiny Eiffel Tower charm too. Susan's mother had dreamed of visiting the tower. When Susan chose it as the story starter, she and her mother would imagine going to France and wearing bright, floral dresses, wide-brimmed hats, and gloves to match. They would pretend to take the elevator to the café on the landing of the Eiffel Tower and order croissants with cheese and sip sparkling water out of crystal champagne flutes. They'd sit on Susan's bed tossing their imaginary floral scarves across their shoulders, clinking their water-beaded glasses, and with a French accent, interject the few French words they knew: "*Tres bien*," "*Merci*," and "*Oui, oui*."

But Susan's favorite charm was the ballet slipper that dangled between the toy poodle (the only dog Susan's father said they would ever own) and the silver locket that had a tiny picture of her mother inside. Sometimes her mother would take off the charm bracelet and slip it over Susan's wrist, turning her arm from side to side so they could hear the silver jingle. Then Susan would hold the ballet slipper and dance it over her lace-trimmed pillow. "I'm a famous ballerina dancing *The Nutcracker* ballet."

"You can be a ballerina," her mother would say, giving her a squeeze. "Or anything you want." Susan would place the bracelet back on her mother's wrist and dream about dancing. Her mother's loving presence was always so soothing.

At the age of five, Susan took ballet lessons around the corner from their home on the Upper East Side, at the 92nd Street YMCA. Years later Susan's mother was with her when she auditioned for and received a coveted spot at the prestigious school of performing arts. "My little gift from God," her mother had said as she threw her arms around Susan. "You can do great things!" Susan could hear the bracelet tinkling gently in her ear.

Susan loved that sound, and it was such a part of her childhood memories. She'd heard it as her mother made pancakes for breakfast, folded laundry, or turned the pages of Susan's favorite bedtime story. "Do you hear the angel's wings flapping?" her mother would say as Susan ran her finger back and forth across the charms like she was stroking a wind chime. Susan would nod and picture her mother with tiny angels flying all around her. "God's angels will always protect you," she would say, and Susan believed her.

But then Susan's mother encountered something so terrible that even the angels didn't protect her. She got breast cancer—it wasn't diagnosed until it had already metastasized to her lungs. In just a few months, Susan's once vibrant mother had wasted away to a fragile shell of herself. Every day seemed to bring another setback or loss for Susan and her mother during those months, and one day, after a particularly difficult trip to the doctor's office, they had been heartbroken to discover that the bracelet was missing.

Susan had searched everywhere, retracing their steps and calling the doctor's office to ask if someone might have turned it in. But it was no use. The bracelet was gone. Undoubtedly it had slipped off her mother's wrist, which was emaciated from the ravages of cancer, radiation, and chemotherapy. Losing the bracelet had brought Susan immense grief. But mostly she grieved because the bracelet's loss seemed to be an ominous portent of greater loss to come.

Indeed, only eight days later, Susan had held her mother's hand at her deathbed. It had pierced her heart to see her mother's wrist without the familiar bracelet. As the woman struggled to breathe, Susan stroked her hair as her mother had stroked hers when she was a child. Between gasps for air, Susan's mother labored to give one final message to her daughter.

"Susan . . . my precious gift from God. You always . . . make me proud. Someday you'll . . . be . . . famous ballerina . . . dancing *The Nutcracker*. And when you are . . . know that . . . I'll be right there with you. I believe . . . in you. I . . . love you. Even when I . . . can't be . . . with you . . ." She pointed up. Susan almost thought she could hear the rush of angels' wings and the jingling of her mother's bracelet.

But wait, that wasn't part of her memory. The sound was pulling her back to the present, to the cab, and the driver who was once again talking to her.

"I found this between the seats in the back of the cab a few months ago. Sure is pretty. I always hoped I'd find the owner, but seems like that would take a miracle. Got a picture of a young woman looks kind of like you. But the part you'll like is the ballet slipper." He held up a shiny silver charm bracelet and extended it toward Susan. "I'd like you to have it—a gift."

Susan's heart pounded wildly, and strong emotions threatened to overwhelm her. It was her mother's bracelet! How could this be? Susan once again heard the faint jingle of the bracelet as she took it reverently from the man's hand. She knew God's angels must be surrounding her. And she knew her mother was with her too—and always would be.

"Happy birthday, Mom," Susan whispered through sudden tears. "Thanks for the gift."

A Mother's Presence

We mothers worry so much about what we say to our children and how we care for them. Yet we often forget that children learn most from just watching us. How do we approach life? Do we move through our days with gratitude, excitement, and energy? Our loving presence shapes our children's hopes and dreams. It gives them the confidence to step out into the world knowing that they can always return to the security of our spirit, even if only through childhood memories.

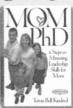